Where She Dances

∽

Michael Jennings

FUTURECYCLE PRESS
www.futurecycle.org

Cover artwork, "Female Figure," ca. 3500-3400 B.C.E., Brooklyn Museum; author photo by Suzanne Shane; cover and interior book design by Diane Kistner; ITC Benguiat Gothic text and titling

Library of Congress Control Number: 2019956353

Published by FutureCycle Press
Athens, Georgia, USA

ISBN 978-1-942371-82-3

For Suzanne, my muse

Contents

A DANCE OF STONE

*For beauty's nothing but the beginning of terror
we are still just able to bear…*

—Rilke *Duino Elegies,*
trans. by Stephen Spender

Ur of the Chaldees, 1958

They are like aliens on the moon, the Americans—
bermuda shorts and cameras, pudgy, pale,
a little queasy from the train ride.
Dust from the storm in the night
has permeated everything they own
down to the skin.
They are not quite certain why they came
and wear the baffled, blinking looks of baby birds.

The hole in the ground is the biggest I've ever seen,
with "evidence of the flood"—a four-foot-wide ribbon
of sand halfway up the sides of an otherwise brown pit
strewn with broken bits of pottery. Local kids, urchins,
scamper down the steep, thin path at breakneck speed
for *rials* and *dinars*. They seem to have sprung up here
without benefit of parents or care. Across
the millennia, I feel the closeness of children
and the terrible price of money.

After a long climb, I am first to reach the summit
of the ziggurat
and so enter the dusky sky of Abraham.
I am 10. My heart is a drum.
I stand at the top of the godforsaken world.

A Man Squatting in the Shade

As if one with the plowed contours of carved rock
where the sunlight has taken centuries
to cultivate its dead, he squats and stares
at the land's long shudder toward the horizon.

Only the one slow hand, fumbling from time
to time among the stones, and the loud bark
of rock on rock echoing from the cliffs
disturb the bright perfection of this day—

the dark face flinching with the contact. What
but the first quick act of murder, half-conceived,
the smooth downward arc of the first chipped rock
splintering the mind, could hold him here
                              where he
survives in a six-foot circle of life—
in the scorpion's country, but in Cain's land.

Cow Skull

This is the land's death mask, the splintered face
into which earth's bodiless distances
bulldozed to a halt,
                     the great brain
ousted by wasp nest, sagebrush thrust
from the caved nostrils.
                     You would think
staring into the round, gaping eye
that nothing could have died so utterly.

On the horizon, the stone town darkens
and turns blue. Soon it too
will fall to ruin—
                     like the honed cheek
of the cow's skull, turning to husk
in the evening air—
                     while dry, birdlike men
come picking their way homeward
over the broken fields.

The Women of the Hills

move slowly through the drifting streets
like the bearers of news from a far country.
Among dry walls, they are the dream's
watery shadows, which on waking
leave only the trickle of sweat
on a burning brow.
                    Yesterday and before yesterday
fall to their province; and when it's hot, like today,
and their feet bleed and grow caked with the road dust
and around them the landscape reels and thrashes
as in a nightmare,
                  they are the bearers of dreams
from the home country, where night is falling,
the wind rising, and where their black *chadora*
have grown ghost-gray,
                    where they are the substance
and the ash and the plunder of men.

The Egg Woman

She has no teeth, and if she cries at all,
it is not with her eyes, for they have gone
beyond the dark reaches of her face
long ago.
         Her attitude is utter blindness,
though she sees perfectly well, crossing our ridge,
eggs cradled in her stolen paint cans, her bent back
dropping behind a boulder, as if feeling her way
far back, down some dark place in the landscape
only she knows.
         And as the locals tell it
(and they are fond of telling it), before the fire,
before the catastrophe that brought down
home, poverty, old age, all in a single
combustible moment,
         she was far the richest whore
in all Khuzistan, with silks and tapestries to boot.

But these are rumors. These hills
are filled with rumors, the muttering of cripples,
the crying of children.

Horse

Here is the relic of Bronze Age glory no teenage boy
can quite shake from his daydream—the lust of Achilles,
the soft curve of haunch that tempts theft
under cover of moonlight beyond neighboring hills.
Alexander's eyes rolled and flashed like horses' eyes.
The Great Khan's standard was a horse's skull.

But this is mere tribal mare, circa 1960, gaunt
as Picasso's horse under a rider thin as shadow.
But spirit still channels through the twin poles of the neck.
Mood plays out in the whim of leaf-shaped ears.
She knows she was made for travel and moves
with the accustomed grace of a dancer

over white flats in liquid blue heat, over red rock
aglow each night from the fires of a hundred oil flares,
on some errand ancient as Ur, tied to death or birth—
whose rider would rather starve than sell her—
whose solemn cheek is a barge prow in the moonlight,
patient on the breathing river—

who mothered the thunder.

Rock Lizard

The lizard puffs his throat in the sun.
Glutted as he is with the white world,
only a sudden darkness
                              makes him stir,
head cock to stab, or else
the whole body rise
in a momentary shuddering poise

before the sudden swift shift
and annihilation
of stone, hill, field and sky
in the soundless flickering of his flight.

And now, downhill, under a flat stone,
where the world forms
and reforms
in the pool of an eye,
                              I enter
again this still kingdom
where I am only
a dark hulk
              come hogging the sunlight.

View of a Wedding: The Fat Man

We've come on horseback deep into the hills
for this, along sand roads hardened by crude oil
and blazing sun.
                I am sitting next to the Fat Man,
intrigued by the watermelon biceps bulging his suit coat
as he crushes beer cans between two fat fingers
at least a decade before the aluminum can's
invention.
            When he finishes one, I hand him another.
"Careful," whispers Khosrow, "when he gets drunk
he kills people."
              The bride is a child about 13
and skinny as a boy. She goes through the ceremony
with the wide-eyed, dutiful look of a kindergarten kid
in a school play.
             The groom, too, looks terrified.
After the vows, they retire to a room to consummate
the marriage while the women trill like cicadas
and the men do the sword dance with crude sticks—
ancient, elaborate, no doubt dangerous.
               Kahbelli, my groom,
who tends my horse like a wet nurse to the crown prince,
and whose village this is, wears the same baggy, brown uniform
he does day in, day out.
            When I ask to take his photograph,
he braces to attention like a palace guard—
stooped, skinny shoulders pulled back, the haggard,
kind face, always with a day's growth of beard,
stern and almost proud.
            When Khosrow proffers
a full 8-ounce tumbler of vodka, he downs it
with a single draft, bows and offers a slight salute,
and begins a little baggy-panted dance—Appalachian
almost, or Ozark.

The music is drum and whiney, reedy horn
that brings the hills down close, that is ghost dance
and night pulse, that lulls the Fat Man to sleep
and brings out the groom with his bloody handkerchief
to a cry that splits the night,
                              vaulting the two drunken
Englishmen into the sword dance ring
for their predictable cornhole parody
that makes the villagers laugh
                              and the Fat Man snore
and night close over us in a blaring of horns.

Fatima's Wedding Dance

Today, of all days, has been called mine. And tonight,
which for four years I lay in fear of, also mine.
I bend, I snap, I bite back tears that what was bought
with years of tears, sweat, labor of my father's hands,
shall not break, shall not snap. Of me they shall speak well.

And if you find my body frail, a small birdlike thing
not fit for love or spoil—the arms thin, the back weak—
you have not seen my father's hands, the bent fingers
reaching like dark claws into this parched and broken soil,
nor do you know the yearning of this heart of hearts—

that, soon, I too will dance the dance the women dance,
wail as they wail, give lands, daughters, into the hands
of those that come—and that my sons, grown tall, shall take
what's theirs—and that I come to dance the funeral dance
of this down-cheeked boy whose dead weight and hands I bear.

So let it not be said I came as lamb to slaughter,
or that for me the young she-goat was brought to slaughter.
My name is Fatima. I bring my father's lands,
and mine is the blood flows back to my father's land.
For me they fly the red kerchief, my mother's daughter!

The Wind-Curved Sandhills

*And make mention of the brother of Aad when he warned
his folk of among the wind-curved sandhills—and verily warners came
and went before and after him—saying: serve none but Allah.
Lo! I fear for you the doom of tremendous day.*
—the Qur'an

First there comes the large rasping voice
among the dunes, and the men moving toward it—
sunbaked, humorless men who stand or squat,
occasionally muttering among themselves.
Today they learn about the pain of generation,
the thanklessness of youth: how a woman
nurtures a man for forty years
and gains nothing; learn, too,
how a dark storm cloud will dissolve
into the thunder of hooves; and how,
after that, villages will stand empty
but for the wind.
                    At noon, food is brought out
on large platters, the water in goatskins.

***

Later, toward evening, a man squats in his tent
speaking as though into his hands. He wants,
somehow, to reach this gaunt, patient woman
who squats and rocks on her heels, nursing a child.

She remains skeptical, incurious—
her dark eyes distant, her face hard.

Suddenly he stops speaking and begins
gouging absurd little stick figures
in the dirt. He has the words wrong, he explains.
He will go listen again tomorrow.

She nods and smiles and goes on suckling the child.
He stares back sheepishly into his hands.
Looking at him now, she may almost imagine
how, in a few years' time, this shy, brooding face
will burst through doors
                           and how the children
crouching inside will scream.

***

It is twilight,
and a man moves quietly among the dunes.
Reaching a ridge,
he kneels down in deep sand.
He thinks he hears a voice.
What he hears
is the wind gnawing the tough tendrils of grass
at the dune's lip.
Taking a handful of sand,
he begins pouring it over his head.
He pours another
and another.
He thinks
the sand is water
or tears
or perhaps even stars.

A Dance of Stone

Whoso ascribeth partners unto Allah hath wandered far astray.
They invoke in his stead only females; they pray to none else
Than Satan, a rebel.... As for those women who are found guilty
Of lewdness...confine them to their houses until death take them.
—the Qur'an

For six long days they have surrounded my house—
these fat, squat men crouching upon their hams,
having their food brought out to them—eating,
leering, and licking their thick fingers. Six
long days. And on the seventh, I shall die.

I can remember how my father knelt
for hours before the stone goddess, a hard man.
And when he took me in his arms and squeezed,
I wished, sometimes, I too were stone. At night
he loved my mother hard. From where I lay,
I'd see her face grow larger and more craven
until, at least, she'd scream. Her face grew calm
then, calm and small, like that of the stone goddess.

The night of the long scream, when the men came
with large, torchlit faces and killed my father,
I didn't cry. My mother screamed and her face
grew large. And he was small then, small and broken
like the stone goddess. But I didn't cry.

And then the men with torches and large faces
took me with them, and, for a time, were kind.
They told me of a strong god who was kind
to women, merciful they said, because
women were weak. And as I grew older,
they came to me at night and brought me gifts
and told me how my breasts grew large. At dawn
they cursed me, saying it was they who were weak.

I grew distrustful then, though never showed it.
I took their gifts: this house, the serving
man they gave me. Agreed, also, to consort
no more with the good women of their tribe,
but only with this single serving man.

And still at night they came to me with gifts
but spoke no more about their strong, kind god.
Once, in the night, one brought my father's goddess—
charred, broken—saying how I might mend her.
I cried then, cried for having once forgotten
how small she was, and broken, and but half
understood—cried in words I hardly understood.
And the years passed. And still at dawn they cursed me.

At last, this six days past, the elders came
and cursed me then in earnest, said my house
was Satan's house and my gods Satan's gods.
They took my goods, my food, the serving man
they'd given. When they left, they locked the door.

I screamed then, tearing at my clothes, my hair.
I clawed great furrows in my face and breasts.
And feeling how my own blood ran, I cursed them—
cursed just to see them there, squatting and leering,
having their food brought out to them. At first
I cursed only in their own blunt, thick tongue;
later, in the smooth language of my father.

At this they laughed and jeered and threw small stones.
I saw their hatred then, their fear, and I screamed
louder and longer, cursed until I fell
exhausted. Then they laughed again and asked
what good my father's stone could do me now.

Becoming calm, I went deep into my house,
far from the shouting and the stones. They fear
this silence, I said, fear my stillness. From me
they want only some mad, lewd dance, not quiet—

they do not want me dead, only to die.
And I took up my goddess, spoke to her
and made her whole, finding what I had half
known, half forgotten—the stone goddess dances.

Tomorrow when they enter into my house,
they shall come quietly, afraid, as if
into a shrine. And I shall dance for them—
dance of my father and my father's people—
a strong dance, a good dance, a dance of stone.

In the Bazaar, the Laying On of Hands

Out of the skull's comic grimace,
cloud-shadow stitchings and touchings of hands,
a flesh-fingering wind, the tongue's reflex
flexing to its heartstring
torturings—
                as in the lightning-bolt
suddenness of mountain, the road below
abruptly liquid and lashing—a face
come up out of a sea of faces, sharper,
larger, like a great boulder, opening
in the oppressive heat—
                        not a cry
so much as a lifted up blackness
out of the belly's pit, a momentary
moronic braying ravaged forever
by the drum-roll haggling of hawkers,
vendors, the donkeys' needle-like hooves
sharpening under the massive heave of their burdens.

Hanoon

Our cook, Hanoon, tells me he is a Chaldean,
displaced by who knows how many migrations,
murders, to come to live in Braim Village
along the river green with date palms,
cool in its dark mud huts even in summer,
though he must ride to our house across
the blazing salt flats on a comic huge bicycle
wearing a pith helmet. His teeth are oddly dark
along the gums, though serving as wire cutters
when he needs them.
                    He wrings the neck of a chicken,
and we laugh to see it scuttle in crazed circles,
crashing into the walls of the compound. So death
is right here with us always, and maybe
we too are crazy chickens.
                    When I am eleven,
we come to dine at his village. He is something
like a Head Man, and we are given *fesenjahn*
that looks like mud and tastes like ambrosia.
We eat from a common bowl with our hands,
and for the first time I feel holy.
                    In the bazaar,
the beggar boys scatter like startled birds
at a single hissing whisper from his lips,
his hands fluttering like quick black bats.
                    For hours
he squats at cards, slapping them down with true
gambler's relish—his big, bare, broad feet,
so quiet as he pads, cat-like, about the house,
planted happily on the wide earth,
his pockmarked face smiling
like a black leopard's.
                    Years later,
we'll lure him with money to another town,

far from his family and tribe,
to live, displaced, among the grim Bakhtiari.
And he will service us, less smiling than before,
and steal our silver; and we will fire him,
and I will know what it is like
to steal a man's joy and pride
and break his heart.

In my dreams, I break bread with him still.

Procession Bearing Food to the Dead

Over dry lips in the stark sun
moves the black tongue—
                      folly of the lizard,
eyes of the dead.
                And we have come
at dawn on slow feet in black cloth,
crowns on our heads,
                  while the date palms widen
like great hands in the low sun
because the darkness becomes us.
                        Because when great wind
stirs at our ankles with the reeds' low whisper
near the bull snake's shadow,
                we become again
the children who move whitely among us—
guided by birds,
          indifferent as angels.

Woman in Purdah

A woman in a black veil. Black for the dead,
veil for the living. A face that in a million years
you will never love. Mandible, zygomatic arch,

orbit and frontal bone. Your fingers will never trace
the contours of this darkness, any more than that of
cloud shadow or the winged blackness among the grass.

Think of ash, coal from the mountain, obsidian
polished like glass, or the hand of moonlight
on dark water.
                But you will not lie down
among the long bones of evening.
                        You will stand,
as you must,
            in the indifferent intimacy of a hot day
like a man trying to remember the age
                    of his dead daughter.

Along the Avenue of Dead Gestures

Surely there have been darknesses
before this one,
                            growing between the doors,
moving as I move
                            down the cobbled streets
full of the vacant eyes, thick thighs and gold teeth
of the women who work them.
                                        Bones rotted before these,
or the round skull of the child froze
in the broad, bloodless face
of the whore.
                    After me, there will come other deaths.
Others will walk home by the back roads.

Heat

Day without plot. Fixtured and fissured. Fractured beyond
    measure.

I have known heat to stretch horizon to horizon
like bright steel—a metal or mica or star-scattered heaven
foundering the mind. Thick-tongued and wordless. White sand
on black brain. Blood rivered in suet. A pocket
picked empty as wind.
                            Nothing moves in such heat,
not lizard or scorpion, sandfly or shadow. Tree
becomes rock, becomes gray husk, becomes
ruinous. Squalor of sand. Numbness of sun.
                                    To squat there,
the stones of your absence in your hands,
is to squat in the center of silence forever.
It is to hold the sun like water in the crumbling of your hands.

***

It is to hold the bright day. Sun. Sand. A dun-colored dog

disappearing into a distance of sun and sand—
humped, slavering. The steady
rise and fall of the four flickering paws
too maniacally silent and concentrated for even
the loose gesture of wind to intrude on.
                              Or a dream of day,
a child's sorrowing and dreaming—aftermath
of that too much excitement. Four boys with baseball bats
who had braved what they knew of the horrors
of the desert, a compound of mad dogs
and oil drums,
                barbed wire and heat,
a dun-colored dog disappearing into desert like a dead wind.

                              ***

It hangs like a daydream of fish in the sun's eye. Fish flying

like birds above the thunder of dynamite, burble of river,
then falling to flotsam. Fish by the armload,
blind, dazed, flaccid as faith. A stench
ripping open the whole length of the gullet of sky
luring foxes and flies.
                    A day I walked in sun,
unstable as the dynamite I carried in a brown paper sack
like an indigestible lunch.
                        And threw. And walked. And threw.
And watched the shards of hillside rise
like torn brains to hang in the hair of scrub trees
while the lizard sang silent in the sun—the blood-
throated lizard, bloated and bragging in the swaggering sun.

***

Or the daydream of glass. White light. Bone light. The sailing
    of glass—

shards of pottery heaped in domes
where ziggurats grew round in wind
and the tombs of kings
stunk with centuries of fox.
                        The sun was a blind, mad eye
carved on an obsidian stairway to heaven
where the fallen bulls of stone
offered their great backs to me to ride
and dust filled the air like glass.
                        Mother's eyes were black fires
as she hurled ashtrays and plates, bowls and crystal
at walls and mirrors. Her voice
was glass breaking. Her breath was ether.
                        The stench of fox,
like the burning of flesh, stayed in my nostrils for days.

***

A dream before I knew you, met you. Though I knew of
    your absence.

I knew of Lydia Cathcart who spread her great thighs
on the Riding Club couch or across
the great outcropped boulders of the desert
for grooms and stable hands.
                               I knew of her husband's
straw-colored, pomaded hair and creased
high-fashion trousers
                    and how her eyes bugged out a little
and spittle formed at the edges of her mouth.
                                Akbar,
who would die in the advanced stages of syphilis,
served our drinks and food, laughed
like a girl, and kissed me when he could.
I knew of your absence. And I dreamed of Lydia Cathcart.

***

And of women on horseback—long shadows in the deep hills.

And one who rode a stallion like a black wind
that even I could not ride,
                              her hair a raven black.
And then the horse who fell and bled for me,
a deep pocket of blood forming between his forelegs
like a breast—
                    a black horse with a girl's mane
and a king's name.
                        And then the dream of women
ridden by men or boys
in the twilit paddock, moving
down the long hill in the long heat, arm
in arm, indifferent to all but the long loneliness
of the first stars rising,
                              the glittering of raw, fierce weapons.

***

And the desert rises then in the twilight. It lifts

its burnt body out of itself. The scabs of its flesh
soften. It sings in its silence like an old woman
and becomes young again.
                              Her sands glitter in moonlight.
Her ridges rise like deep rivers entering the sea of stars.
Her foxes find new stealth,
                              their fur bristles.
Snakes slither from dark dens with eyes like stars
and tongues like the singing of stars.
                                        This is the clarity
of fire.
        This is the clarity of the long bones of the hills
rubbing together like the thighs of the long woman
buried among them.
                        This is death.
This is the white-hot crotch of death, blue as a diamond.

***

And Gafoor smokes his hookah with yellow eyes. Rocks

and claps his thighs. Dreams himself. Stinks of horse,
stinks of women, stinks of the sun and the sun's lies,
the long ride.
        And the round stones of the moonlight
are the hunched backs of the night's feeders
who rise and walk—
            or the arched bellies of the night's
eaten. Who do not get up. Who turn on themselves
like sculpture. Blue stones.
        And the tarantula
rising like smoke
        sings to his green-eyed mate
under the arched light of her dark sting
and dances there in the round light.
            Long night.
The yellow-eyed. Soft-thighed. Torn and turning.

***

And then shard-light in the broken east and the stones' cry—

the huddled bones,
carcass and carcass. Confession of sand,
celebration of wind.
                        And bright blood blooms in the desert
as the blind white fish
flounder from withered pond
to withered pond
where once the river flowed hard
in the moonlight.
                        Achilles died
that Odysseus might live—the heartless heart
succumbing to the body's stealth,
                                        the moon-fired fox,
skulking and singing, meeting the dawn's dead eye.

***

O daughter of days. Mother of nights. If I have sought women

as the sun
seeks water,
                eye
in eye,
        tear
              and muscle,
                          forgive me the long chains'
shackle and shackle. Forgive me the great bull-bones
of the world in the sun
                        and hold me now in the implacable
pallor of your gaze, this improbable poise
of full moon at dawn's edge—
                          bone-song,
                                    wind-haunt,
voice of the fathers
and the father of voice—
                        bring back
the great wind,
              sing me the singing,
                                the great song—

O blood of the mothers who labored long!

Inner Sanctum

Anood and Matrood Jassemzahdi
have long since moved from their home by the courts
to the low mud huts of Braim Village.
Years have passed since our tennis days,
and I am crossing the barren flats for the last time,
feeling the heat rise through the soles of my shoes,
seeing it waver, silvery-blue, as the black-green
date palms near the river grow
imperceptibly closer.
                        The heat is an odd familiar.
It holds me in its palm like a puppet.
The dizzying distance of the flats to the north
could be glare ice, polar smoke, or the timeless lake
it once was.
                        Miles and miles and miles
the mind sails as the feet plod
a few hundred yards. Sunstroke, heatstroke,
are states of mind almost religious, the body
spooling off into darkness.
                        The narrow
dark paths of the village are welcoming
labyrinthine passageways, silvery-blue
eyes of trachoma flickering in the shadows.
My hands grope for a few cool coins
to assuage the heat of conscience.
                        The doorway
is there—a few low-ceilinged rooms
fanning off from the courtyard, palatial
by village standards—the swept dirt floors,
open spigot in the courtyard,
and the chador-draped figures of Mother
and Sister, two silent hearth goddesses
of the cave-cool gloom, mourners of a life
more ancient than I can imagine.

                              In just such a room
Christ, the wanderer, must have had his weary feet bathed
with just such sure strong hands as theirs.
                              And for his crown
he must have worn just such camel thorns
as I have idly scuffed in coming—
                              anything like a rose

being rare in these parts.

Old Mountains

There were mountains in the old place,
the place of old bones, and the mountains
were like bones, only browner, sandstone,
though sometimes bleached pale as bones.
And dark goats moved among them,
and the people who grew out of them
were like goats, small and dark
and quick when the sun was not pure
poison, moving about their business,
which was not our business, theirs
being soil, which there wasn't much of,
ours being oil, which came out of the ground
by the ton and snaked through the hills
and desert in pipelines inevitable
as the azure, steel sky itself. Perhaps
they were not real mountains so much
as upthrust foothills, craggy plateau
a man or goat could climb in a day,
stand at the top of, and feel Moses
come down from.
                They were holy mountains,
and under the holy mountains was oil
that sometimes still made bushes burn
or the Red Sea part for the islands
of deep-bellied freighters pregnant
with crude.
        And if they were not mountains,
they were at least the high steppes
of the horsemen, grown ghostly with time;
and my sleeper's body slept among them;
and my dreamer's body, which was only smoke
from village chimneys in winter, or the black
eyes of the skulls of their huts in summer,
saw the quick shimmering emerald of the fields

and crevices in spring, the flash of the bright-dressed
girls of the waterhole, their ankle bracelets
saucy as the glitter of crime in Salome's eyes,
and the black eyes under the black wind
of the black *chadora*
billowing around the husks of crones.
They were the sacred mountains camped
at our outskirts while our fathers
mined oil from beneath them and hardly
saw them.
         But their graves sang to us
in the evenings, and the thin smoke
of their cook fires rose like ghosts,
and they lay down with us in our dreams
like beasts, breathing and patient.
                   "Ours,"
we thought, as the Persian blue sky
swaddled their shoulders, as the black
night sky lay down on their backs
with its pinprick stars. They rose
like continents in the black sea
of nightfall, then rose again like the skulls
of sacrificial beasts in the dawn. And perhaps
our white mothers heard them and started
drinking harder, savaging the servants,
quarreling with our sad-sack fathers.
Distracted in the midnight, they paced cold tiles,
their bare feet lisping the hours—
ethereal, haughty, silken whisperings.
And the mountains were theirs, too,
and the dirty hands of the servants
who needed such scolding. Some absence
lurked in their eyes like the shadows
of mountains, among the coffee klatches
and beer-swilling mornings.

But we
were the children of the mountains,
and they entered us as easily as sky,
as easily as night; and what they showed us
was fire and shadow, dancers under the worn moon.
And we saw how time moved in ripples toward the horizon,
shuddering under the noonday sun. They moved
in us like the spirits of Alexander or Herod,
Nebuchadnezzar, Ashurbanipal, Xerxes
or Artaxerxes—slow fires
in the waking midnight.
                        And our incongruous
fathers waited at the bus stop—white,
short-sleeved shirts, clip-on ties
and crew cuts. They talked of Oklahoma
or L.A., Atlantic City or Baton Rouge,
but never of the bleached mountains
on the hem of whose skirts they stood,
dazed in the morning light. Their gaze
was too calculated, the sheaves of paper
in their briefcases too diagrammatic
and impersonal. Children of the Depression,
their souls had suffered foreclosure.
They had bankers' eyes.
                        They are mostly
dead now, copies of *Forbes Magazine*
strewn on the night table. And we
who were children of the mountains
search nightly on the News for glimpses
of the pale, pitiless sleepers—there
behind the reporter with blank banker's eyes,
beyond the rolling dust of tanks, bomb blasts
and squalor, the rubble of apocalypse.
We have joined the absent ones.
Nothing there now remembers us
but the mountains
                        etched behind our eyelids.

WHERE SHE DANCES

During the dismal months the soul sat shrunken and lifeless,
but the body took the straight path to you.
The night bellowed.
By stealth we milked the cosmos and survived.

—Tomas Transtromer "Firescribbling"

Where She Dances

Purple jaguar midnight
of lost imaginings—ebony, jet,
obsidian lakes of fire—
hers are the drumbeat spanking of bare
hard feet, the far off wafting of laughter.

Come dance with the daughter
of ragtag summer. See the turn
of her fiery wrist. Moon
paints her shadow. Sun
cannot find her. The fierce stars

bring her to bliss.
Once she was tree, trembling in moonlight.
Once she was river
tied down by her hair.
Once she was wind, once she was breath—

now only flame
in the flare
of a pupil,
a delicate rustle's
velvety purr.

When the River Flutters

her wings, she is no longer the Amazon
floating the crescent moon as her navel,

she is your shadow rising to meet you.
The night-silk mountains bend close.

Something in the lisping silence grieves,
exalts, dies its thousand deaths.

Your body is also a river with wings,
with talons, a place of betrayals

where shadowy gods, horned
or with twisting serpents for hair,

are drowned, torn to shreds,
then rise again into stars.

Tomorrow, at dawn,
something shaggy will come down,

peering out from the night-drugged leaves,
dazzled by the spokes of new sun.

Pythoness

You want her to unravel your future,
make time stand still,
take the pinch of your skin
off.
    But how dry the whisper of her coils,
ton over ton of slow muscle
like molten lava.
                    Her split tongue hisses,
emptying your skull like an eggshell.
Your fate is calamitous—
reckon your chances.
Bring only the candle of yourself
into the cave of unmaking.
                        Slide between smooth stones.

Peering, lidless, yellow eyes.

Her Mermaid Dream

What should she make of the dream-shattered sea
lipping her breasts,
forging her thighs—
herself nonetheless
remote as a jewel, dry in the wetness,
miraculous.

Again and again she flies in the mirroring well—
dazzling jungle bird
of the sea's fetch, angelfish fluttering
ogreish,
maw full of seaweed—
                                        whose wild wail
whispers to your ear like a seashell.

The Eye of the Mountain

is inward and honeycombed,
aswirl with the nectar and knowledge of ages—

what the mouth knows
but the tongue has forgotten—

glacially calm in its weeping—
its tears the blood that becomes milk.

Her Dalliance

Between her fingers
the plucked stalk of your brainstem
blossoms,

petal after petal, in the empty air.
Between her toes
Tigris and Euphrates divide

and multiply. She loves you,
she loves you not.
Perhaps you are the pinprick rain

on the sheer face of an autumn lake.
Perhaps you are snow.
She is dreaming of crossroads

and you are the emptiness.
She is playing with dolls
and you are the mad muttering.

She is gossiping by the well
and you are the strewn fieldstones,
lidless eyes of the desert

waiting for rain. Her indecision
is delicious with cunning.
The mountains heave. Your leaves shiver.

When She Makes Mountains

she paints them shadow-dancing,
        rivers their flexions,
weaves the drapery wind. Dozes.

        Crosses into dream-space
with long-thighed stepping, her sleep-heat
        burnishing the low hills.

Out of them come women for water,
        bright as flowers, a dozen Salomes
with braceleted ankles and hard brutal feet

        who crouch on their haunches
under the thick scent of limes, their mud village
        creviced above them,

its brown face among the cliffs
        immobile as a blind man's.
She breathes them her gossip,

        whiskers their thighs,
puts the wheels of their hips
        in slow motion. Jars

grow from their heads, jars
        in the shape of women
heedless in May, the time of new grasses.

Sometime Before Words Perhaps

your arm moved—
a glitter of small hinges.
Or was it your leg,
its calculated unwinding?

I was asleep, say,
or lost in thought.
I heard your blood,
though, how it sang,

and I felt your cloud-shadow
coming, crossing my face.
I looked—
you were full of yourself

dancing. I looked—
you were the waterfall of yourself
dancing. I looked—
your breath drank my eyes.

I listened—your feet drummed
shut my ears. I groped,
but your skin turned fingers
to spider webs.
                Sometime,
out of the dark of my body,
I spoke.

Today Perhaps the Lizard

who lies down in his own shadow,
inventing the sun through half-closed eyes,
feels his skin, thickening with years,
grow nervous as water.
Perhaps he just feels lucky.

You keep coming back like a dream.
Your hips make light shiver,
make me peer up silly-sideways
like an old dog
to watch the bonfire of your bones.

Night's coming, though.
The sky-blue water
of your eyes will turn dark
then. Stars will come out.

Tomorrow
you will come and go again
like a river—
your bright bones
                    stealing my shadow.

At Twilight

Fatherless among the animals, I wake in the half-light,
sinless as a June bug, pure as Narcissus.
I am what I look at.
The leaves see me and know my smell.
What I touch touches me back.

I cannot know whether I am the flower
or the flower of the flower
or just smooth water
reflecting tree more ravishing than tree,
flower more wayward than flower,

when your witch-light comes like gossamer
brushing my cheek.

The Trees Too

lean
as if seeing themselves,
as if hearing, there in the silence,
the crumbling bark, strewn branches, torn roots
collapsing into the huge patience
of leaves—
            brooding or dancing,
homeward or exiled.
                Out of such silence,
a long dark cry.
Water has fallen. It is dreaming a sky.

Soundings

Something stays in the mind just beyond knowing
or speaking, but there, all the same, like dark water.

A man can walk out five ways into wind
and come back a tree or snow leopard,

but a woman is different, opens like a sea,
dons no disguises, kisses what she needs,

takes what the moon sends her. Her knees hold horizons.
She lets the shaggy land lie down there to drink.

Once

(with some thefts from Simon Behbehani)

I came to you as if from a far country.
The night was not quite in your eyes,
but the evening smoke and the roses of your skin
met in purple shadows.

I came through the vague veiled streets
toward some clarity or hunger.
You were my fire in the moth-light,
my confessor.

You danced the stars blind under the witching moon.
I crawled in your darkness like the tapping beetle.
Our mouths met.

Dawn in the desert is a million gold butterflies.
I lived there once among broken stones,
husks of bodies,
a tale of death and deaths
and women turned to salt
under stubborn hummocks of black cloth.

We grow old like the cracking clay
of forgotten rivers.
Soon no one will remember our voices
or the glancing light of our tremulous
tremors.

Was it the wind I came on,
lipping your waters,
combing the sunlight scarves across your throat?

So often now we are tired,
and old women I once knew speak harshly
behind the curtain,
and the mud of the riverbank
squelches under their feet.

I came through bulrushes over moon-glazed bayous,
and our bodies became snake-dancing
cranes,
feathery cries.

We cannot love each other forever
except as the stars do,
all flame and nothingness.

Our skins will grow worn and frail
as papyrus leaves,
locust wings.
May the burden of pain bring lightness.

We lie down to take flight
like the desert sand under the scour of wind.

I came like a sea eagle out of the sun's eye
to whirl you, talon in talon,
down the roller-coaster sky.

I met your gaze in the forest of being.

The rest was just history.

Acknowledgments

Poems in *A Dance of Stone* originally appeared in *The Georgia Review, Prism International, Kansas Quarterly, The Louisville Review, Vanderbilt Review, Four Quarters,* and *Era,* and several were also included in *Crossings: A Record of Travel, New and Selected Poems,* Lamar University Literary Press (2016).

And from *Where She Dances* (largely inspired by images created by painter and photographer Darryl Hughto), the first eight poems originally appeared in *Corresponding Voices, an Anthology of Contemporary Poetry* described as "a dialogue among poets across cultures," Point of Contact Publications (2002).

My gratitude to all.

About *FutureCycle Press*

FutureCycle Press is dedicated to publishing lasting English-language poetry books, chapbooks, and anthologies in both print-on-demand and Kindle ebook formats. Founded in 2007 by long-time independent editor/publishers and partners Diane Kistner and Robert S. King, the press incorporated as a nonprofit in 2012. A number of our editors are distinguished poets and writers in their own right, and we have been actively involved in the small press movement going back to the early seventies.

The FutureCycle Poetry Book Prize and honorarium is awarded annually for the best full-length volume of poetry we publish in a calendar year. Introduced in 2013, our Good Works projects are anthologies devoted to issues of universal significance, with all proceeds donated to a related worthy cause. Our Selected Poems series highlights contemporary poets with a substantial body of work to their credit; with this series we strive to resurrect work that has had limited distribution and is now out of print.

We are dedicated to giving all of the authors we publish the care their work deserves, making our catalog of titles the most diverse and distinguished it can be, and paying forward any earnings to fund more great books.

We've learned a few things about independent publishing over the years. We've also evolved a unique, resilient publishing model that allows us to focus mainly on vetting and preserving for posterity poetry collections of exceptional quality without becoming overwhelmed with bookkeeping and mailing, fundraising activities, or taxing editorial and production "bubbles." To find out more about what we are doing, come see us at www.futurecycle.org.

The FutureCycle Poetry Book Prize

All full-length volumes of poetry published by FutureCycle Press in a calendar year are considered for the annual FutureCycle Poetry Book Prize. This allows us to consider each submission on its own merits, outside of the context of a contest. Too, the judges see the finished book, which will have benefitted from the beautiful book design and strong editorial gloss we are famous for.

The book ranked the best in judging is announced as the prize-winner in the subsequent year. There is no fixed monetary award; instead, the winning poet receives an honorarium of 20% of the total net royalties from all poetry books and chapbooks the press sold online in the year the winning book was published. The winner is also accorded the honor of being on the panel of judges for the next year's competition; all judges receive copies of all contending books to keep for their personal library.

www.ingramcontent.com/pod-product-compliance
Lightning Source LLC
Chambersburg PA
CBHW070012100426
42741CB00012B/3217